DEEP GLIMPSES

BETWEEN THE ROCK AND A HARD PLACE

Five Biblical Roles for Transformative
Conflict Engagement

P.J. ALLAN

Published by Deep Glimpses
www.deepglimpses.com

Print ISBN: 979-8-9928260-6-7
E-book ISBN: 979-8-9928260-7-4

Printed in the United States

CONTENTS

INTRODUCTION

I can still remember the day I was sitting in my office, feeling completely overwhelmed and way over my head. Let me explain the situation, so you can understand what was happening.

We started our church with about seventeen people and met in the local high school for six years. After purchasing some land, we began our first building project. Nothing fancy, just a practical meeting place with offices and a couple classrooms. It was a pole barn. It didn't take long for us to outgrow that space and we experienced a season of what I called the F.O.G. —meaning the Favor Of God! Other pastors would ask me what we were doing to cause this growth and I would honestly answer, "I have no idea!" I always felt God was blessing the work, not because of us, but rather in spite of us stumbling and fumbling around trying to keep up with what was happening.

During the following six years on the property, there were seven additional building projects. Because of the growth we experienced, I was invited to serve on our organization's International Board of Directors. Later, they appointed me to be a District Supervisor overseeing fifty-two churches, while still pastoring our local church. Meanwhile, my wife and I added an in-law suite to our home to take care of her aging parents in their late eighties. We had a staff of twenty-two, and with that came some help, but it also came with some confusion over differing ideas and a variety of ministry philosophies. Many suggestions they made seem to offer a better option on how things should be run . . . if they were the pastor. In addition to all that were the many weekly tasks of sermon preparation, staff meetings, counseling sessions, hospital visits, and officiating weddings and funerals, to name a few. I knew I was in way over my head.

So, back to that memorable day in my office. I was sitting at my desk with my head in my hands praying. I will never forget the pressure I was feeling. It was overwhelming. I knew I couldn't keep all the plates in the air spinning around me and they were about to crash. There was intense pressure coming from every direction and I remember crying out to the Lord: "God, I feel like I'm stuck between a rock and a hard place." His answer came swiftly and to the point. Within a moment, I comprehended the depth of it. He said, "And that's exactly where you belong." That is not what I expected to hear. I was hoping for something more empathetic, maybe a little comforting, a little consoling.

Accompanying His word came the idea of how a car's shock absorber functions. During my teenage years, I worked at a gas station, where I frequently performed oil changes working underneath vehicles. The shock absorber is a cylindrical-shaped compression unit that takes the shock from the tire hitting a chuck hole or bump and absorbs the impact. It's positioned between the frame and the axle, so those seated in the car will not get the full jolt of the impact. It absorbs the shock, like being between a rock and a hard place. He was showing me that our place, as believers in this world, as followers of Jesus, is to be that shock absorber. The Rock is Jesus Christ, and the Hard Place is the world. We stand between conflicting worldviews, broken relationships, destructive attitudes, and even principalities of darkness. The problem here is that most of us try to avoid these types of conflicts. Please believe me when I say I completely understand. I mean, who wants to put their finger in that fan? Right?

Christ intentionally positioned Himself on that cross between the sins of the whole world and the righteousness of a Holy God and absorbed the shock so that we, by grace, can have an acceptable, accessible entrance into His glorious kingdom. He absorbed the wrath of God on Himself for us and offers complete atonement for all our sins.

Baby Steps

We'll first examine why conflict avoidance betrays our calling (Ezekiel 22:30), then explore how encountering God's holiness re-orients us (Isaiah 6). Finally, we'll unpack the five roles of Ambassador, Mediator, Peacemaker, Advocate, and Intercessor—each modeled by Christ Himself.

CHAPTER 1: STAND IN THE GAP

And the word of the LORD came to me, saying, "Son of man, say to her: 'You are a land that is not cleansed or rained on in the day of indignation.' The conspiracy of her prophets in her midst is like a roaring lion tearing the prey; they have devoured people; they have taken treasure and precious things; they have made many widows in her midst. Her priests have violated My law and profaned My holy things; they have not distinguished between the holy and unholy, nor have they made known the difference between the unclean and the clean; and they have hidden their eyes from My Sabbaths, so that I am profaned among them. Her princes in her midst are like wolves tearing the prey, to shed blood, to destroy people, and to get dishonest gain. Her prophets plastered them with untempered mortar, seeing false visions, and divining lies for them, saying, 'Thus says the Lord GOD,' when the LORD had not spoken. The people of the land have used oppressions, committed robbery, and mistreated the poor and needy; and they wrongfully oppress the stranger. So I sought for a man among them who would make a wall, and stand in the gap before Me on behalf of the land, that I should not destroy it; but I found no one. Therefore I have poured out My indignation on them; I have consumed them with the fire of My wrath; and I have recompensed their deeds on their own heads," says the Lord GOD.

—Ezekiel 22:23–31

I think we can relate to the times the prophet Ezekiel is describing here. A time of total corruption and violation of the Word of the Lord. He is describing priests, prophets, and leaders in a criminal cover-up for their own dishonest gain, leaving destruction with widows and orphans in their aftermath. In verse 30, we read how God sought for a man who would stand up against this culture, and raise the standard that had long been rejected and ignored.

I believe that today we are at a critical season for true believers. For many, their faith has been a place to hide. There is a legitimate time for our faith to be an essential refuge for us, but the times are changing and the world needs to see our faith rise into action. I am not talking about protests or boycotts. I am referring to an inner development that finds expression in our day-to-day lives—right where we live. A form of boldness and confidence that does not avoid conflict, but instead enables us to address and resolve issues effectively. We need to represent the kingdom of God through the *peace of God* and the *wisdom of God*. I know this seems like a high call, but isn't that what we are called to in the first place? The days of "patty-cake" Christianity must give way to an awakening of the true members of Christ's body to rise and shine. Why else would we need the Armor of God that Paul talks about, if not to enter the fray?

Our nesting, comfortable lives have been a terrible distraction from actual spiritual growth and engagement. It seems we are all too willing to accept what should be deemed "unacceptable" in light of God's Word, those things which deserve a strong opposition or even rebuke. But many choose the alternative of safety and security by not opposing current trends. They are satisfied with status quo in this temporary and transitional realm. Instead, let us recognize we are here to represent God's eternal kingdom, which endures beyond this life and carries everlasting significance. As we have opportunity to make a difference, let us not ignore this need any longer. No longer will we be lulled by shallow or pseudo expressions of faith. We need to get real, to get deep, and to begin walking out our own transformation. Then, and only then, will we make a difference in the world.

Is it that we are ill-prepared, ill-equipped, or just cowardly? These questions are not meant to bring condemnation, but rather seeking an objective cause, so that we together, might discover a cure. What are we missing? I would like to make a few observations that may help us find a direction that will awaken our souls.

OUR OWN UZZIAH CAN GET IN THE WAY

Let's look at Isaiah chapter 6, verse 1.

> *In the year that King Uzziah died, I saw the Lord sitting on a throne, high and lifted up, and the train of His robe filled the temple.*

It is of great significance we understand the first seven words of this chapter: "In the year that King Uzziah died."

King Uzziah, also known as Azariah, was an effective king, and under his rule, Judah was prosperous. Uzziah was a successful military leader who expanded Judah's territory and fortified Jerusalem. He built towers in Jerusalem at the Corner Gate, the Valley Gate, and fortified them. He also built towers in the wilderness and dug many cisterns, because he had large herds, both in the Shephelah and in the plain. Under Uzziah's reign, Judah experienced economic prosperity. He promoted agriculture and viticulture (cultivating grapevines), and he had farmers and vinedressers in the hills and in the fertile lands. Uzziah was also known for his innovations in military technology. He made devices in Jerusalem, invented by skillful men, to be on the towers and the corners, to shoot arrows and hurl great stones.

Despite his successes, Uzziah's pride led to his downfall. He entered the temple of the Lord to burn incense on the altar of incense, a duty reserved for priests. When the priests confronted him, he became angry, and as a result, he was struck with leprosy. He lived in a separate house, excluded from the temple of the Lord until his death.

When we succeed, we often focus on our achievements and rely on our own abilities and accomplishments. But once our self-sufficiency is removed, that is when we are able to look up to see the Lord who rules and overrules. Consider what might be your Uzziah? What represents your stability and confidence?

When I was just beginning to turn my life over to Jesus, I had a friend who knew me before my conversion. Her name was Hope and I became like a big brother to her. She had no family in the area, so she was somewhat adopted by my parents. She actually stayed at their home more than anywhere else. As I began to grow in Christ and His salvation, I tried often to share the Lord with her. She resisted the idea and held on to blind traditions she had since she was a child. So in between getting her a job and helping her find her own place to live, I would bring her to church where the gospel was clearly preached, and the power of God was manifested. Still, she resisted and defiantly rejected the idea of turning her life over to Christ Jesus. I finally moved her into her own apartment, and she secured her new job. The day I was leaving from moving in the last piece of furniture, I told her that I would not be available any longer and wished her the best. The next Sunday, she came to church and gave her heart to the Lord. So after the service, I approached her with a surprised look on my face and asked her what just happened. She said she always felt like I would be there for her, and when I said that she was on her own, she realized she needed Jesus and turned to Him with her whole heart. All that time, I thought I was helping, when in reality I was hindering. I must have been like Uzziah in her eyes.

HOLY, HOLY, HOLY, WOE

Back to Isaiah 6.

> *Above it stood seraphim; each one had six wings: with two he covered his face, with two he covered his feet, and with two he flew. And one cried to another and said: "Holy, holy, holy is the LORD of hosts; The whole earth is full of His glory!" And the posts of the door were shaken by the voice of him who cried out, and the house was filled with smoke.*
>
> *So I said: "Woe is me, for I am undone! Because I am a man of unclean lips, And I dwell in the midst of a people of unclean lips; For my eyes have seen the King, The LORD of hosts."*
>
> *Then one of the seraphim flew to me, having in his hand a live coal which he had taken with the tongs from the altar. And he touched my mouth with it, and said: "Behold, this has touched your lips; Your iniquity is taken away, And your sin purged." (v. 2–7)*

Once we are able to see beyond our temporary dependencies, that is when we will see the Lord high and lifted up in the glory and majesty of His eternal domain. In fact, I believe this is the primary lack for many who proclaim Christ: We are without a clear, unhindered vision of where He is today. Many still only see Him on the cross or even in a manger, but we cannot comprehend that He has entered His heavenly realm, and is now seated in glory at the right hand of the Father. He is high above all principalities and powers and has been given ALL AUTHORITY in heaven and on earth. He is the Lord of Hosts, the Mighty God, the Everlasting Father, the KING OF KINGS AND THE LORD OF LORDS. He Reigns!! Only when we comprehend, envision, or experience His glory are we like Isaiah, willing to lay down our temporary interests to avail ourselves, to step up and be willing to be used for His purposes. That is exactly what happened to Isaiah in chapter 6, verse 5. Along with seeing the holiness of God, we also see our own uncleanness, and for many, they disqualify themselves because of it instead of dealing with it. Now Isaiah was a prophet of God. He heard the Word of the Lord and would declare His words, but this was different. Once you see yourself compared to His holiness, His brilliance, and His power, you see yourself differently as well.

I remember growing up, we would spend holidays at my aunt's house. They had a bigger house, and it would facilitate our family getting together much easier. She had an all-white miniature poodle named "Snowball." For the holidays, she would put bows in the dog's hair and paint its nails with polish. Let's just say it was a festive time. This dog really was as white as white can be, or so I thought. It was wintertime, and I will never forget the sight. We'd had a heavy snowfall over the past few days, and at one point, she let her dog out in their fenced in backyard. I remember taking a peek out the patio doors and thought I saw what looked like a big grey rat. It was all the way against the back fence. Then my aunt opened the door and called her dog. It started running toward the house. It was Snowball! When it was in the house, it looked clean and bright, but compared to the fresh snow it was grey and dingy.

We can see ourselves as doing all right and compared to each other, we can still hold our own. But once we are in the presence of the all-powerful, holy God, we will say like Isaiah, "Woe is me."

Another point to be made here is that when you are before God and you see the actual condition of your heart and soul, you realize there is nothing you can do to make yourself look better. You cannot cover it up. You cannot change yourself. You are naked and open before Him and the state of your soul is, in and of itself, wrecked . . . but there is hope and a powerful provision made by God to bring about the change you need. Notice, this provision came from heaven's side. It was a part of the altar of God, the place of sacrifice. Jesus who came from heaven, took on flesh and became one of us to carry our sins on the cross. We can only be justified by the work of God, and there is nothing we can do for ourselves. In Christ alone, I place my trust.

READY & WILLING TO STEP UP

Isaiah 6 continues.

> *Also I heard the voice of the Lord, saying:*
> *"Whom shall I send,*
> *And who will go for Us?"*
> *Then I said, "Here am I! Send me." (v. 8)*

The prerequisite for being sent by God is to see Him in His glory and to be cleansed at His altar. Then, we are in position to say, "Here am I, send me." It is not just about being busy for God or simply volunteering at the church. Those may be places He will call you to serve, but you had better be able to do what you are doing *for Him and for His glory.* There are times when we have an authentic encounter with the Holy Spirit to the point where we are moved and inspired. We desire to serve Him; we desire to follow His will, and that is a valid call and response. But unfortunately, instead of hearing more of the specifics in our calling, we are often not willing to wait for God to further lead us in our daily lives. We approach our pastor or leader and tell them we want to do something to serve Jesus. While trying to keep their "in-house" ministries moving, pastors will at times place us somewhere we were never really called to serve. At first, we are glad to be used, but if that service is not accompanied by the blessing and anointing of God, we slowly begin to dry up inside. Don't get me wrong, God can still bless those times and teach us something in them. But if you are still listening to Him, He may be wooing you to serve somewhere else.

When we first started our church, we needed help everywhere. Home Groups, nursery, children's church, youth groups, worship team, sound/tech, ushers/greeters . . . you get the picture. I remember asking people who wanted to serve to join in at the place where we had our most current need. In first Peter we read:

> Coming to Him as to a living stone, rejected indeed by men, but chosen by God and precious, you also, as living stones, are being built up a spiritual house, a holy priesthood, to offer up spiritual sacrifices acceptable to God through Jesus Christ.
>
> —1 Peter 2:4-5

I actually would put a person in a position and within a short amount of time, they wanted to serve somewhere else. Picture building a house and putting a living stone in the windowsill. You turn around, and the stone moved over to the door frame. That's exactly what it felt like until I realized that it was not about filling holes with volunteers, but rather helping everyone find their place in God's building, even if it was outside our four walls. That was one of the times our church grew exponentially, and we enjoyed seeing individuals filled with strength, while serving where God had gifted them.

Probably the most honest statement I have ever heard was when the vice president of our organization was offering me a position to serve on our International Board of Directors. This is how he said it: "I don't know what God's will is for your life, but we have a plan." Of course, it was said in humor, sort of. It is that innocent, subtle shift that can ultimately grow into a counterfeit, long-term position, but only if we continue to ignore the unction of the Holy Spirit in our lives.

GETHSEMANE

Where the cross is the manifestation of Christ's surrender to the will of His Father, Gethsemane is the place where Jesus wrestled with His reality and brought it into a compliant partnership with His Father's plan. We may never be called to a level of sacrifice as to die a martyr's death as part of God's plan for us, but we all must associate and pass through our own Gethsemane. That is the place we surrender our will to His will . . . and it should happen more than one time.

> Then He said to them all, "If anyone desires to come after Me, let him deny himself, and take up his cross daily, and follow Me. For whoever desires to save his life will lose it, but whoever loses his life for My sake will save it."
>
> —Luke 9:23–24

Paul writes of his own Gethsemane in 1 Corinthians 15:31, when he pens: "I die every day!"

YES, LORD

Did you know that you cannot say, "NO, LORD"? Because either the "no" disqualifies the Lord, or the "Lord" disqualifies the no. If He is, in fact, Lord of your life, then your life belongs to Him, and your response must always and only be, "YES, LORD!"

> *Or do you not know that your body is the temple of the Holy Spirit who is in you, whom you have from God, and you are not your own? For you were bought at a price; therefore glorify God in your body and in your spirit, which are God's.*
>
> *—1 Corinthians 6:19-20*

Reflecting on my years in ministry, saying, "Yes, Lord," opened unexpected doors. It is about submission to His lordship and a willingness to be used for His glory, rooted in thankfulness for all He has done for us. God is performing miracles, transforming lives, restoring souls, and inviting people to come to Him. It is an honor for us to be called into a partnership with His work . . . Yes, Lord! This really is the first step. It starts with a willingness to step in and not step aside. This is the major pivot that can turn an isolated, insecure, and fearful existence into an active, vital, and dynamic catalyst for change. It is not just jumping into the fray, looking for trouble. It is watching and waiting on the Lord for those appointed times —whether by proximity or relationship —that we are sovereignly placed in the middle of an opportunity to contribute constructively. What I'm wanting to offer here are at least five biblical roles or positions that can equip you specifically for bringing legitimate construct to those stuck between a rock and a hard place. Believe me, once you understand these modes of operation, you will be better equipped and have a solid footing in effectively approaching some of the conflicts you previously avoided. So let's take a look at these defined roles, so we can help those stuck between a rock and a hard place.

CHAPTER 2: FIVE BIBLICAL ROLES

After personally being overwhelmed in my office that day, I wanted to find biblical examples of those in similar tense spots. That led me to see common characteristics in these varied situations. I realized other tense situations, defined and funneled down into these five positions. Of course, I am sure there are other applications, but these five seemed to offer me the sure footing I needed when approaching conflict or tensions. These five roles are AMBASSADOR, MEDIATOR, PEACEMAKER, ADVOCATE, and INTERCESSOR. You may already understand how each of these roles depict filling a gap during conflicting times. We will develop each of these roles to see their unique attributes and characteristics. This will help you approach difficult situations to discover a solution when you find yourself between a rock and a hard place.

Here, we will look at just a few biblical examples in both the Old and New Testament of each of the five roles. As we compare these examples, you can see how easy it would be to fulfill other roles at the same time, depending on how you look at them. The truth is, they were all between a rock and a hard place, but if you look closer, you can discern a subtle nuance that features one role stronger than another. Also, there is a short-term view and a long-term view. We will consider Joseph as our first biblical example of an Ambassador. In the short-term, Joseph served as Pharaoh's ambassador to preserve the Egyptian nation, but the long-term shows that he was also Jacob's Ambassador, and he saved the nation of Israel from the famine as well. Again, our intention is not to limit our application of these roles as "official" or "exclusive" expressions. Nor should we attempt to identify in one particular role over another. Each are situational and fluid. You may find yourself moving from the position of an Ambassador to an Intercessor and end as a Peacemaker, all at the same time. The important thing is by defining and understanding these five roles, you will have a platform by which you can operate as well as know your primary mission.

AMBASSADOR

An ambassador is a high-ranking representative who acts as an official envoy for their country, organization, or cause. Traditionally, ambassadors represent their governments in diplomatic missions, working to maintain relationships with foreign nations. They help with negotiations, political discussions, and cultural exchanges to promote cooperation between countries. Beyond politics, the term is also used more broadly. A brand ambassador, for example, promotes a company's image or products, while a goodwill ambassador may work to raise awareness for social or humanitarian causes.

Picture the number of ambassadors from all over the world having to negotiate with countries who are contrary or in direct conflict with one another. To hold your post on foreign soil and not compromise your country's best interest is a good example of a rock and a hard place. You may not think of it this way, but the movie *Dances with Wolves* tells the story of a single soldier stationed at an abandoned outpost. He was alone and surrounded by a local Sioux tribe. The story shows how difficult it can be to stand in an isolated territory, while interacting with the apparent enemy. The distinct lines separating us are often blurred and we are tempted to compromise our responsibilities as an ambassador.

This is actually a very understandable scenario, but let's look at the same situation in our day-to-day lives. In our workplace or our school, we are called to be an Ambassador for God's kingdom. It is much easier to do this in a church setting where everyone is on the same side, but what happens when we leave the comfort of like-minded people and find ourselves in foreign territory? The lines can get blurred and our position compromised.

> *A wicked messenger falls into trouble,*
> *But a faithful ambassador brings health.*
>
> —*Proverbs 13:17*

Joseph

If there was ever anyone who was not looking to be placed in a conflict, it was Joseph. His brothers hated him and reported his faked death to their father, Jacob, which broke his heart. Joseph was sold into slavery, then falsely accused by his master's wife, and thrown into prison. Yet, throughout this turmoil, God was developing a deep strength and gifting him with divine wisdom. Because of his ability to interpret dreams, he was brought before the Pharoah himself to interpret a troubling dream. Okay, right there is a tough spot to be put in. You better have the goods, the gift, the correct answer. I believe at this juncture, Joseph was a "peacemaker." Pharoah was troubled and conflicted, and by the wisdom of God, his heart was put to rest bringing peace into this situation. We will look into this more a little later.

As I alluded to earlier, Joseph was assigned by Pharoah to prepare during the seven prosperous years for the upcoming seven-years of famine. Joseph's life as an ambassador is evident in his representation of God's will, his diplomatic mediation between cultures, his pursuit of reconciliation, his stewardship of resources for the greater good, and his role as a type of Christ. His story illustrates how an ambassador operates with integrity, wisdom, and a heart for others, always pointing to a higher authority—God Himself. Joseph's life serves as a model of an ambassador's conduct in both spiritual and practical dimensions.

Paul

If you were to look through Acts chapters 13–28, you would see that Paul functioned as an ambassador. God called him to be an apostle to the Gentiles (non-Jews), a mission that required him to cross cultural and religious boundaries to share the message of Christ. When God spoke to Ananias concerning Paul, He said:

> But the Lord said to him, "Go, for he is a chosen vessel of Mine to bear My name before Gentiles, kings, and the children of Israel. For I will show him how many things he must suffer for My name's sake."
>
> —Acts 9:15–16

Paul speaks of his own calling:

> But when it pleased God, who separated me from my mother's womb and called me through His grace, to reveal His Son in me, that I might preach Him among the Gentiles, I did not immediately confer with flesh and blood, nor did I go up to Jerusalem to those who were apostles before me; but I went to Arabia, and returned again to Damascus.
>
> —Galatians 1:15–17

Paul did not choose to go up to Jerusalem to meet with the elders, but rather separated himself to seek God alone. He had to re-learn everything he knew from his synagogue training and have the Holy Spirit tutor him in new revelation. As an ambassador for Christ, Paul represented the authority and message of Jesus, proclaiming reconciliation with God through faith in Christ's death and resurrection. He carried the gospel to diverse regions, adapting his approach to connect with different audiences. In Athens, Paul spoke at the Areopagus, tailoring his message to the Greek philosophers by referencing their altar to an "unknown god" and quoting their poets to explain the one true God (Acts 17:22–31). This demonstrates his skill as an ambassador to contextualize the gospel, while remaining faithful to the message of gospel, acting as a representative of Christ in a foreign cultural setting.

Again, Paul directly refers to his role as an ambassador in 2 Corinthians 5.

> *Therefore, if anyone is in Christ, he is a new creation; old things have passed away; behold, all things have become new. Now all things are of God, who has reconciled us to Himself through Jesus Christ, and has given us the ministry of reconciliation, that is, that God was in Christ reconciling the world to Himself, not imputing their trespasses to them, and has committed to us the word of reconciliation.*

Now then, we are ambassadors for Christ, as though God were pleading through us: we implore you on Christ's behalf, be reconciled to God. For He made Him who knew no sin to be sin for us, that we might become the righteousness of God in Him.

—2 Corinthians 5:17–21

Here, we see once again, the main objective of an ambassador is to negotiate reconciliation. The ambassador will stand in the middle of conflict in the hope to navigate the contending parties to reconcile. Can you think of a time when you were used to help reconcile a conflict? As believers, our goal is not only reconcile personal differences between the offended and the offender, but also to help them to be reconciled to a right standing with God.

For anyone desiring to serve in this capacity as an ambassador, the following scripture must apply if we are to be successful in our service.

Stand therefore, having girded your waist with truth, having put on the breastplate of righteousness, and having shod your feet with the preparation of the gospel of peace; above all, taking the shield of faith with which you will be able to quench all the fiery darts of the wicked one. And take the helmet of salvation, and the sword of the Spirit, which is the word of God;

*praying always with all prayer and supplication in the
Spirit, being watchful to this end with all perseverance
and supplication for all the saints—and for me, that
utterance may be given to me, that I may open my
mouth boldly to make known the mystery of the gospel, for which I am an ambassador in chains; that in it
I may speak boldly, as I ought to speak.*

—Ephesians 6:14-20

Contemporary Example of an Ambassador: The School Board Diplomat

Scenario:

A local school board meeting erupts over proposed curriculum changes. Angry parents demand removal of books addressing racial injustice, claiming they're "divisive." Teachers argue the materials are essential for teaching critical thinking. The superintendent is paralyzed by the pressure.

Ambassador Action:

Elena, a Christian parent and former teacher, steps to the microphone: "As a mother, I share your desire to protect our children. As an educator, I know these texts help students process hard truths safely. What if we form a parent-teacher committee to review materials together? We could create study guides that align with our community's values while preparing kids for the real world."

Why This Embodies an Ambassador:

- Represents a higher kingdom
- Doesn't side with either faction; appeals to shared values (child safety + quality education)
- Reframes the conflict
- Shifts from "ban vs. defend" to "how can we collaborate?"
- Offers a third way
- Proposes a solution (committee + study guides) that honors both concerns
- Models reconciling language
- Uses "we" instead of "you" and "what if" instead of "you must"

The thing that is different in the role of an Ambassador is that you are taking a stand as the primary representation of the sovereign you are representing. You are in a foreign land, but not just to "get along." You are there with an assignment or at least a stronger position than a neutral one. The Apostle Paul, on Mars Hill in Acts 17:22–23, is a good example. Paul was walking among the idols of the foreign gods in Athens and came across one inscribed, "TO THE UNKNOWN GOD." Paul took that opportunity to declare that he was there to make known to the men of Athens who this unknown god was. Paul turned a neutral environment into a platform to declare the gospel in the context to his surroundings.

MEDIATOR

A mediator is a person, group, or entity that acts as an intermediary or neutral third party to help facilitate communication, negotiation, or resolution of a conflict between two or more parties. The role of a mediator is to assist in finding a mutually acceptable solution without imposing a decision, unlike a judge or arbitrator. Mediators are commonly used in disputes, diplomacy, or business negotiations to promote dialogue and understanding.

A mediator is a NEUTRAL third party. Like a telephone line connecting a conversation, it serves as a means to clarify each party's conflicts in order to help reconnect them together. You will find this role in marriage counselling or in helping friends bridge a misunderstanding. In a workplace dispute, a mediator might help employees resolve interpersonal conflicts by encouraging open communication.

Moses

Moses is an amazing example of a Mediator. From the beginning of his calling, he stood between Egypt's Pharoah and the ten plagues, then between Pharoah and the Israelites, and again he stood between God and his promised people as he met with God on Mount Sinai. The courage and wisdom he shows is an inspiration.

> Now when the people saw that Moses delayed coming
> down from the mountain, the people gathered together

to Aaron, and said to him, "Come, make us gods that shall go before us; for as for this Moses, the man who brought us up out of the land of Egypt, we do not know what has become of him."

And Aaron said to them, "Break off the golden earrings which are in the ears of your wives, your sons, and your daughters, and bring them to me." So all the people broke off the golden earrings which were in their ears, and brought them to Aaron. And he received the gold from their hand, and he fashioned it with an engraving tool, and made a molded calf.

Then they said, "This is your god, O Israel, that brought you out of the land of Egypt!"

So when Aaron saw it, he built an altar before it. And Aaron made a proclamation and said, "Tomorrow is a feast to the LORD." Then they rose early on the next day, offered burnt offerings, and brought peace offerings; and the people sat down to eat and drink, and rose up to play.

And the LORD said to Moses, "Go, get down! For your people whom you brought out of the land of Egypt have corrupted themselves. They have turned aside quickly out of the way which I commanded them. They have made themselves a molded calf, and worshiped it and sacrificed to it, and said, This is your god, O Israel, that brought you out of the land of Egypt!' " And the LORD said to Moses, "I have seen this people, and indeed it is a stiff-necked people! Now therefore, let Me alone, that My wrath may burn hot against them and I may consume them. And I will make of you a great nation."

Then Moses pleaded with the LORD his God, and said: "LORD, why does Your wrath burn hot against Your people whom You have brought out of the land of Egypt with great power and with a mighty hand? Why should the Egyptians speak, and say, 'He brought them out to harm them, to kill them in the mountains, and to consume them from the face of the earth'? Turn from Your fierce wrath, and relent from this harm to Your people. Remember Abraham, Isaac, and Israel, Your servants, to whom You swore by Your own self, and said to them, I will multiply your descendants as the stars of heaven; and all this land that I have spoken of I give to your descendants, and they shall inherit it forever.'" So the LORD relented from the harm which He said He would do to His people.

—Exodus 32:1–14

Moses served as a mediator between God and His rebellious people. He reminded God of His promises to Israel and that it was for His name's sake, that He should not destroy them in His wrath.

Paul

If you want to see a masterful example of a mediator, it has to be the book of Philemon. Paul, while in prison, leads a runaway slave to Christ, Onesimus, who became a help to him. In the course of their relationship, Paul discovered that he ran away from someone Paul had known, whose name was Philemon. In this book of Scripture, Paul is writing to Philemon in the hopes of restoring their broken relationship, but the intricacies and nuances of Paul's negotiations are pure genius.

In an effort not to ruin the artistry of Paul's mediation, please allow me to put the whole letter here. It's one chapter, 25 verses long. I hope you enjoy this eloquent diplomacy of Paul's mediation.

> *Paul, a prisoner of Christ Jesus, and Timothy our brother, To Philemon our beloved friend and fellow laborer, to the beloved Apphia, Archippus our fellow soldier, and to the church in your house: Grace to you and peace from God our Father and the Lord Jesus Christ.*
>
> *I thank my God, making mention of you always in my prayers, hearing of your love and faith which you have toward the Lord Jesus and toward all the saints, that the sharing of your faith may become effective by the acknowledgment of every good thing which is in you in Christ Jesus. For we have great joy and consolation in your love, because the hearts of the saints have been refreshed by you, brother.*

Therefore, though I might be very bold in Christ to command you what is fitting, yet for love's sake I rather appeal to you—being such a one as Paul, the aged, and now also a prisoner of Jesus Christ—I appeal to you for my son Onesimus, whom I have begotten while in my chains, who once was unprofitable to you, but now is profitable to you and to me.

I am sending him back. You therefore receive him, that is, my own heart, whom I wished to keep with me, that on your behalf he might minister to me in my chains for the gospel. But without your consent I wanted to do nothing, that your good deed might not be by compulsion, as it were, but voluntary.

For perhaps he departed for a while for this purpose, that you might receive him forever, no longer as a slave but more than a slave—a beloved brother, especially to me but how much more to you, both in the flesh and in the Lord. If then you count me as a partner, receive him as you would me. But if he has wronged you or owes anything, put that on my account. I, Paul, am writing with my own hand. I will repay—not to mention to you that you owe me even your own self besides. Yes, brother, let me have joy from you in the Lord; refresh my heart in the Lord.

Having confidence in your obedience, I write to you, knowing that you will do even more than I say. But, meanwhile, also prepare a guest room for me, for I trust that through your prayers I shall be granted to you.

Epaphras, my fellow prisoner in Christ Jesus, greets you, as do Mark, Aristarchus, Demas, Luke, my fellow laborers. The grace of our Lord Jesus Christ be with your spirit. Amen.

—Philemon 1:1–25

Paul weaves a tapestry of tensions around Philemon between commending him, reminding him that he owes his life to Paul, and including a subtle threat that he will be visiting him for accountability's sake, all compiled into a successful welcome mat for Onesimus to come home.

Contemporary Example of a Mediator: The Neighborhood Restorer

Scenario:

Two neighbors, Mrs. Chen (elderly widow) and the Parkers (young family), are in bitter conflict. Mrs. Chen complains the Parkers' tree roots are damaging her garden wall. The Parkers resent her "constant nagging" and loud complaints to other neighbors. Both have stopped speaking, and the homeowners' association is threatening fines.

Mediator Action:

Rev. Alvarez (local pastor who knows both families) intervenes, with separate listening sessions and solution for both sides.

To Mrs. Chen: "I hear your fear about your garden's safety — that wall is your late husband's legacy."

To Parkers: "I understand that you feel unfairly judged as 'bad neighbors' when you're new parents doing your best."

He reframed the core Issues: "This isn't about trees or walls; it's about security (Mrs. Chen) and welcome (Parkers)."

He facilitated a joint solution, organizing a Saturday where:

- The Parkers paid for arborist consultation (proving roots weren't damaging walls).
- Mrs. Chen hosted lemonade for their toddler.
- The church youth group repaired Mrs. Chen's garden beds.

During his mediation, he also:

- Listened beneath the words to the heart's cry.
- Refused to take sides, but named all truths
- Designed solutions where everyone gained dignity
- Sealed reconciliation with shared action

This is the sacred work of a mediator, who is navigating conflict between a rock and a hard place! As followers of Jesus in a dark and dying world, it is our obligation and calling to step into these types of conflict as faithful mediators, to bring the light of Jesus, and His peace that passes all understanding.

PEACEMAKER

Blessed are the peacemakers,
For they shall be called sons of God.

—*Matthew 5:9*

We must make an important distinction at the beginning of this section. Blessed are the PEACEMAKERS, not PEACEKEEPERS. There is a world of difference between these two. A peacekeeper will do anything to keep everybody together and getting along. Peacekeepers do not want any trouble and at times are willing to compromise convictions for the sake of peace itself or at least maintaining a compliant posture. A *peacemaker* works to bring a *solution* to the conflict, not just avoid conflict altogether. It can be messy and noisy. It can seem to amplify the conflict before resolving it. In the Old West, the Colt Single Action Army (SAA) revolver was introduced in 1873 by Colt's Patent Firearms Manufacturing Company. It earned the nickname "Peacemaker" because it became a symbol of law and order during the tumultuous period of the American frontier. The revolver was widely used by lawmen, cowboys, outlaws, and soldiers, and it played a significant role in shaping the history and mythology of the Wild West. A gun being a peacemaker? Let us just say it brought the solution to irreconcilable differences. Now, of course, this is not what we are talking about in our role as a peacemaker. Our goal is to bring the wisdom of God into a conflict and rectify it with power, yes, but that power is the Holy Spirit and life.

31

For though we walk in the flesh, we do not war according to the flesh. For the weapons of our warfare are not carnal but mighty in God for pulling down strongholds, casting down arguments and every high thing that exalts itself against the knowledge of God, bringing every thought into captivity to the obedience of Christ, and being ready to punish all disobedience when your obedience is fulfilled.

—2 Corinthians 10:3–6

Abigail

Abigail was the wife of a wealthy land owner in the time of King David's reign. Her husband was a hard and difficult man and rubbed many people the wrong way. Considering the culture of this time, women were subjected to control and, at times, abuse. The men ruled, and women were to be subservient and, if necessary, cast away. What Abigail did was courageous and, at the same time, violated many of the norms of her day, but God saw her heart and used her as a peacemaker by avoiding the king's wrath.

Now there was a man in Maon whose business was in Carmel, and the man was very rich. He had three thousand sheep and a thousand goats. And he was shearing his sheep in Carmel. The name of the man was Nabal, and the name of his wife Abigail. And she was a woman of good understanding and beautiful appearance; but the man was harsh and evil in his doings. He was of the house of Caleb.

When David heard in the wilderness that Nabal was shearing his sheep, David sent ten young men; and David said to the young men, "Go up to Carmel, go to Nabal, and greet him in my name. And thus you shall say to him who lives in prosperity: Peace be to you, peace to your house, and peace to all that you have! Now I have heard that you have shearers. Your shepherds were with us, and we did not hurt them, nor was there anything missing from them all the while they were in Carmel. Ask your young men, and they will tell you. Therefore let my young men find favor in your eyes, for we come on a feast day. Please give whatever comes to your hand to your servants and to your son David."'

So when David's young men came, they spoke to Nabal according to all these words in the name of David, and waited.

Then Nabal answered David's servants, and said, "Who is David, and who is the son of Jesse? There are many servants nowadays who break away each one from his master. Shall I then take my bread and my water and my meat that I have killed for my shearers, and give it to men when I do not know where they are from?"

So David's young men turned on their heels and went back; and they came and told him all these words. Then David said to his men, "Every man gird on his sword." So every man girded on his sword, and David also girded on his sword. And about four hundred men went with David, and two hundred stayed with the supplies.

—*1 Samuel 25:2-13*

A Peacemaker recognizes the offense.

Now one of the young men told Abigail, Nabal's wife, saying, "Look, David sent messengers from the wilderness to greet our master; and he reviled them. But the men were very good to us, and we were not hurt, nor did we miss anything as long as we accompanied them, when we were in the fields. They were a wall to us both by night and day, all the time we were with them keeping the sheep. Now therefore, know and consider what you will do, for harm is determined against our master and against all his household. For he is such a scoundrel that one cannot speak to him."

—*1 Samuel 25:14-17*

A Peacemaker is willing to pay the price to make peace.

Then Abigail made haste and took two hundred loaves of bread, two skins of wine, five sheep already dressed, five seahs of roasted grain, one hundred clusters of raisins, and two hundred cakes of figs, and loaded them on donkeys. And she said to her servants, "Go on before me; see, I am coming after you." But she did not tell her husband Nabal. So it was, as she rode on the donkey, that she went down under cover of the hill; and there were David and his men, coming down toward her, and she met them. Now David had said, "Surely in vain I have protected all that this fellow has in the wilderness, so that nothing was missed of all that belongs to him. And he has repaid me evil for good. May God do so, and more also, to the enemies of David, if I leave one male of all who belong to him by morning light."

—1 Samuel 25:18–22

A Peacemaker humbles themselves.

Now when Abigail saw David, she dismounted quickly from the donkey, fell on her face before David, and bowed down to the ground. So she fell at his feet and said: "On me, my lord, on me let this iniquity be! And please let your maidservant speak in your ears, and hear the words of your maidservant."

—1 Samuel 25:23–24

A Peacemaker brings the wisdom of God.

Please, let not my lord regard this scoundrel Nabal. For as his name is, so is he: Nabal is his name, and folly is with him! But I, your maidservant, did not see the young men of my lord whom you sent. Now therefore, my lord, as the LORD lives and as your soul lives, since the LORD has held you back from coming to bloodshed and from avenging yourself with your own hand, now then, let your enemies and those who seek harm for my lord be as Nabal. And now this present which your maidservant has brought to my lord, let it be given to the young men who follow my lord.

—1 Samuel 25:25–27

A Peacemaker is willing to initiate and take responsibility.

Please forgive the trespass of your maidservant. For the LORD will certainly make for my lord an enduring house, because my lord fights the battles of the LORD, and evil is not found in you throughout your days. Yet a man has risen to pursue you and seek your life, but the life of my lord shall be bound in the bundle of the living with the LORD your God; and the lives of your enemies He shall sling out, as from the pocket of a sling. And it shall come to pass, when the LORD has done for my lord according to all the good that He has spoken concerning you, and has appointed you ruler over Israel, that this will be no grief to you, nor offense of heart to my lord, either that you have shed blood without cause, or that my lord has avenged himself. But when the LORD has dealt well with my lord, then remember your maidservant."

—1 Samuel 25:28–31

A Peacemaker receives a blessing.

Then David said to Abigail: "Blessed is the LORD God of Israel, who sent you this day to meet me! And blessed is your advice and blessed are you, because you have kept me this day from coming to bloodshed and from avenging myself with my own hand. For indeed, as the LORD God of Israel lives, who has kept me back from hurting you, unless you had hurried and come to meet me, surely by morning light no males would have been left to Nabal!" So David received from her hand what she had brought him, and said to her, "Go up in peace to your house. See, I have heeded your voice and respected your person."

Now Abigail went to Nabal, and there he was, holding a feast in his house, like the feast of a king. And Nabal's heart was merry within him, for he was very drunk; therefore she told him nothing, little or much, until morning light. So it was, in the morning, when the wine had gone from Nabal, and his wife had told him these things, that his heart died within him, and he became like a stone. Then it happened, after about ten days, that the LORD struck Nabal, and he died.

So when David heard that Nabal was dead, he said, "Blessed be the Lord, who has pleaded the cause of my reproach from the hand of Nabal, and has kept His servant from evil! For the Lord has returned the wickedness of Nabal on his own head."

And David sent and proposed to Abigail, to take her as his wife. When the servants of David had come to Abigail at Carmel, they spoke to her saying, "David sent us to you, to ask you to become his wife."

Then she arose, bowed her face to the earth, and said, "Here is your maidservant, a servant to wash the feet of the servants of my lord." So Abigail rose in haste and rode on a donkey, attended by five of her maidens; and she followed the messengers of David, and became his wife.

—1 Samuel 25:32–42

I imagine most wives would be very reluctant to step beyond their abusive husband in order to remedy his ill-tempered decisions. Abigail risked everything in order to save the lives of her workers and her husband. She executed respect and dignity to show honor to King David and his request. We see that her efforts were not in vain and the reward far outweighed the chances she took, though she didn't know it at the time. God sees the heart.

Barnabas

Barnabus is an incredible example of a Peacemaker. Paul had a reputation of persecuting and arresting Christians and throwing them into jail. He was there at the time when Stephen was stoned to death. Paul himself held the cloaks of those doing the stoning. Now, all of a sudden, the apostles heard that Paul was now one of them. That was a big jump and they were justified in their caution and concern. It was Barnabas who stood up for Paul and put his own reputation on the line for the early church to accept this powerful new convert into their fold.

> And when Saul had come to Jerusalem, he tried to join the disciples; but they were all afraid of him, and did not believe that he was a disciple. But Barnabas took him and brought him to the apostles. And he declared to them how he had seen the Lord on the road, and that He had spoken to him, and how he had preached boldly at Damascus in the name of Jesus. So he was with them at Jerusalem, coming in and going out. And he spoke boldly in the name of the Lord Jesus and disputed against the Hellenists, but they attempted to kill him. When the brethren found out, they brought him down to Caesarea and sent him out to Tarsus.

—Acts 9:26–30

Barnabus also acted as a Peacemaker in his own conflicts with Paul in ministry.

Now when Paul and his party set sail from Paphos, they came to Perga in Pamphylia; and John, departing from them, returned to Jerusalem.

—Acts 13:13

Then after some days Paul said to Barnabas, "Let us now go back and visit our brethren in every city where we have preached the word of the Lord, and see how they are doing." Now Barnabas was determined to take with them John called Mark. But Paul insisted that they should not take with them the one who had departed from them in Pamphylia, and had not gone with them to the work. Then the contention became so sharp that they parted from one another. And so Barnabas took Mark and sailed to Cyprus; but Paul chose Silas and departed, being commended by the brethren to the grace of God. And he went through Syria and Cilicia, strengthening the churches.

—Acts 15:36–41

Some may be surprised that Barnabas acted as a Peacemaker during this "sharp" contention between himself and Paul, after John Mark abandoned them in Perga and went back to Jerusalem. Paul could not let it go and no longer trusted John Mark, while Barbabas still believed in him and was willing to give him another chance—so much so that he preferred to support John Mark and actually parted ways with Paul.

The thing I like about this illustration is that sometimes the only way to bring peace is to walk away. There is a legitimate time to recognize that the opposing conflict is not ready to reconcile. That is why we must follow the unction of the Holy Spirit as to when to press in or when to step back. Again, the interesting long-term results were quite different, as later in 2 Timothy, we see Paul asking for Mark to join him. This is why we cannot force reconciliation no matter how much we desire to see it. We may just know that it is not going to happen now and we transition into an intercessory role, until we see the breakthrough.

> *Only Luke is with me. Get Mark and bring him with you, for he is useful to me for ministry.*
>
> *—2 Timothy 4:11*

Contemporary Example of a Peacemaker: The Worship War Uniter

Scenario:

A small-town church fractures over music. Older members (led by Helen, seventy-eight) demand hymns only: "Anything else dishonors tradition!" Young families (led by Jason, twenty-eight) push for modern worship: "We're losing our kids to churches with guitars!" Both sides threaten to leave. The pastor is overwhelmed.

Peacemaker Actions:

Marie (a forty-five-year-old nurse and choir member) steps in: She halts the escalation:

- Interrupts a heated business meeting: "What if our 'worship war' is actually grief? Some mourn fading traditions; others mourn missing loved ones who left. Can we honor both?"

She creates common ground:

- Hosts a "Story Behind the Song" potluck where older saints share memories of how "Great Is Thy Faithfulness" sustained them in hard times and younger members explain how "Reckless Love" helped them through depression.

She engineers a creative solution, proposing a "Blended Remix":
- Hymn Renewal Project: Youth band records acoustic versions of hymns.
- Modern Hymn Sundays: Once a month, older pianists accompany new songs rewritten in hymn meter.

Outcome:

- No one left; attendance grew by 15 percent.
- Helen and Jason co-lead the music committee.
- A teen confesses: "I finally understand why 'It Is Well' matters."
- The "remix" isn't compromise—it's fusion where both traditions gain new life.

Biblical Backing

We read in Ephesians 4:3: "Make every effort to keep the unity of the Spirit through the bond of peace." Marie prioritized a unity over stylistic "victory." If the goal is to win, we may be focusing on the wrong objective. If the goal is to bring the peace of God and brotherly reconnection, it will look different. An interesting observation as we look in the rear-view mirror of history is the effect of David playing his harp had on the tortured soul of King Saul. In Samuel 16:23, Saul's torment, being soothed through David's music, prefigures Christ's peace. This is the peace we are contending for, not just to stop arguing, but a "calm, godly solution." The specific analogy of the body of Christ found in 1 Cor. 12:12–26, is between the older saints (the church's memories) and the youth (its feet & energy), needing each other.

ADVOCATE

An Advocate uses their voice and influence to protect the marginalized, leveraging privilege for justice and amplifying silenced voices. In the book of Esther, we see a powerful demonstration of the role an advocate, as portrayed through this story of God's wisdom, protection, and sovereignty.

Esther

Esther used her lofty position as queen to influence the king, to show favor to her people, while risking her own life in the process. Like the earlier example of Paul's letter to Philemon, Esther is amazing in her artistic approach to win the king's favor against his trusted advisor, Haman. An enemy to the Jewish people, Haman convinced the king to pass a law that would eradicate the Jewish people from the land.

Mordecai raised his cousin Esther as his own daughter. He protected her until she came of age and was selected to become the next queen for Ahasuerus, a great king over 127 provinces. When Mordecai learned of this new law that would annihilate his people, he demonstrated his great grief by wearing sackcloth and ashes. In Esther 4:10–14, we read:

> *Then Esther spoke to Hathach, and gave him a command for Mordecai: "All the king's servants and the people of the king's provinces know that any man or woman who goes into the inner court to the king, who has not been called, he has but one law: put all to death, except the one to whom the king holds out the golden scepter, that he may live. Yet I myself have not been called to go in to the king these thirty days." So they told Mordecai Esther's words.*

And Mordecai told them to answer Esther: "Do not think in your heart that you will escape in the king's palace any more than all the other Jews. For if you remain completely silent at this time, relief and deliverance will arise for the Jews from another place, but you and your father's house will perish. Yet who knows whether you have come to the kingdom for such a time as this?"

—*Esther 4:10–14*

It was here the words, "for such a time as this," were first written. These words have since become a reference used to confront the times of our sovereign assignments in life. They describe a moment of destiny and primary purpose, a summation moment that encapsulates everything that has happened to us and has brought us to a monumental opportunity. Queen Esther did not miss or ignore this most profound assignment and "stepped up" to become an advocate, leading to the deliverance of her people. Take a moment to read the full story in Esther chapters 4 through 7 and appreciate the elegant way Queen Esther turned the favor of the king to her from Haman, delivered her people, and ultimately caused Haman, the enemy of God's people, to face the gallows he had built for the Jews.

Peter

In Acts 10, we are told of a Centurian named Cornelius, a devout man who feared God, gave alms to the people, and prayed to God always. At one time, he had a vision of an angel from God telling him to send for Simon Peter in Joppa and told him where he could find him.

As he sent his men to Joppa, Peter was on the roof having his own vision from the Lord. He was shown heaven opened and a sheet dropping down to earth. In it were all kinds of creatures that were forbidden in the dietary laws of the Jews. A voice came to him and said, "Rise, Peter, kill and eat." But Peter said, "Not so, Lord! For I have never eaten anything common or unclean," (Acts 10:14). This was done three times and then the sheet went back up to heaven. As Peter was pondering the vision and its meaning, the men from Cornelius came, and the Holy Spirit told Peter to go with them. As they arrived at Cornelius' home, they found it was filled with his friends and relatives waiting to hear Peter. In verses 34–43, Peter shares the gospel message, but the Holy Spirit interrupted his message:

> While Peter was still speaking these words, the Holy Spirit fell upon all those who heard the word. And those of the circumcision who believed were astonished, as many as came with Peter, because the gift of the Holy Spirit had been poured out on the Gentiles also. For they heard them speak with tongues and magnify God. Then Peter answered, "Can anyone forbid water, that

these should not be baptized who have received the
Holy Spirit just as we have?" And he commanded them
to be baptized in the name of the Lord. Then they
asked him to stay a few days.

—Acts 10:44–48

I don't know that we can fathom how radically this changed everything. Previous to this moment, the disciples believed that the gospel was for the Jews, and now God was filling the Gentiles with His Spirit as well! Peter commanded them to be baptized in the name of the Lord, but he had some explaining to do back in Jerusalem.

Now the apostles and brethren who were in Judea
heard that the Gentiles had also received the word of
God. And when Peter came up to Jerusalem, those of
the circumcision contended with him, saying, "You
went in to uncircumcised men and ate with them!"

—Acts 11:1–3

Peter went on to reiterate the sequences that led him to experience this breakthrough and how the Holy Spirit had orchestrated all of it.

If therefore God gave them the same gift as He
gave us when we believed on the Lord Jesus
Christ, who was I that I could withstand God?"
When they heard these things they became silent; and

they glorified God, saying, "Then God has also granted to the Gentiles repentance to life."

—Acts 11:17–18

Peter stood as an advocate for the Gentile believers and convinced the elders in Jerusalem to accept and praise God for His amazing grace.

On a side note, think about the experience Peter had with a vision being shown to him three times, then having the men from Cornelius standing at the gate and the Holy Spirit telling him to go with them, then experiencing a house full of Gentiles being filled with the Holy Spirit. Surely this truth must have been branded on his soul and nothing could cause him to doubt, right?

But in Galatians 2 we read about Paul confronting Peter.

Now when Peter had come to Antioch, I withstood him to his face, because he was to be blamed; for before certain men came from James, he would eat with the Gentiles; but when they came, he withdrew and separated himself, fearing those who were of the circumcision. And the rest of the Jews also played the hypocrite with him, so that even Barnabas was carried away with their hypocrisy. But when I saw that they were not straightforward about the truth of the gospel, I said to Peter before them all, "If you, being a Jew, live in the manner of

Gentiles and not as the Jews, why do you compel Gentiles to live as Jews?

—Galatians 2:11–14

I point this out just to show you the humanity God is patiently working with. Peter soon forgot the position he took supporting the Gentiles and cowered when the leaders came from Jerusalem. God is longsuffering toward us and willing to work, as long as it takes, to transform us into the likeness of Jesus. Be encouraged with the times you lose ground. He's not finished with us! We are all a work in progress.

Contemporary Example of an Advocate: The Hospice Healer

Scenario:

Nurse Maria notices her elderly patient Mr. Davies (terminal cancer) is heavily sedated around-the-clock. His distant children insist: "Keep Dad pain-free at all costs!" But Maria observes:

- He's denied lucid moments to reconcile with family
- Aggressive morphine risks hastening death
- Hospital protocol prioritizes "patient comfort" over holistic care

Advocate Actions:

- Evidence Gathering: Tracked sedation cycles showing no pain spikes during reduced doses

- Researched palliative ethics: "Unnecessary sedation can deprive patients of final meaningful moments."
- Family Intervention: Met with resistant children. "Your love for your dad is clear. But what if 'pain-free' isn't the same as 'peace-filled'? Yesterday, at lower meds, he smiled hearing your childhood photos described. We could try 'comfort pauses'—clear intervals for connection, with meds ready if needed."
- Systemic Push: Petitioned hospital ethics board to add "lucid interval" options to end-of-life plans.

Outcome:

- Mr. Davies shared cherished memories with grandchildren in his final days.
- Children reconciled an estranged sibling during shared visiting hours.
- Hospital adopted "Comfort Pause Protocol" for terminal cases.

Key Advocacy Principle

True advocates kneel beside the broken, before they stand against systems. Their strength flows from seeing the "image of God" in the ignored and fighting until others see it too. It takes a strong sense of conviction and even a calling to stand against what appears to be an outnumbered situation with courage and wisdom. This is especially true in a culture where those qualities are undervalued and made to appear counterculture.

INTERCESSOR

An Intercessor is someone who stands in the gap between God and others, pleading for mercy, justice, deliverance, or blessing on their behalf. It is a spiritual role rooted in selfless advocacy, often involving prayer, fasting, and deep burden-bearing.

Abraham

To me, this exchange between Abraham and the Lord is hilarious. Now, of course, this is a serious and significant issue concerning the destruction of a city. But I just picture God's patience and longsuffering toward us in this haggling that Abraham initiates.

> And the LORD said, "Because the outcry against Sodom and Gomorrah is great, and because their sin is very grave, I will go down now and see whether they have done altogether according to the outcry against it that has come to Me; and if not, I will know."

> Then the men turned away from there and went toward Sodom, but Abraham still stood before the LORD. And Abraham came near and said, "Would You also destroy the righteous with the wicked? Suppose there were fifty righteous within the city; would You also destroy the place and not spare it for the fifty righteous that were in it? Far be it from You to do such a thing as this, to slay the righteous with the wicked, so that the

righteous should be as the wicked; far be it from You! Shall not the Judge of all the earth do right?"

So the LORD said, "If I find in Sodom fifty righteous within the city, then I will spare all the place for their sakes."

Then Abraham answered and said, "Indeed now, I who am but dust and ashes have taken it upon myself to speak to the Lord: Suppose there were five less than the fifty righteous; would You destroy all of the city for lack of five?" So He said, "If I find there forty-five, I will not destroy it." And he spoke to Him yet again and said, "Suppose there should be forty found there?"

So He said, "I will not do it for the sake of forty."

Then he said, "Let not the Lord be angry, and I will speak: Suppose thirty should be found there?"

So He said, "I will not do it if I find thirty there."

And he said, "Indeed now, I have taken it upon myself to speak to the Lord: Suppose twenty should be found there?"

So He said, "I will not destroy it for the sake of twenty."

Then he said, "Let not the Lord be angry, and I will speak but once more: Suppose ten should be found there?"

*And He said, "I will not destroy it for the sake of ten."
So the LORD went His way as soon as He had finished
speaking with Abraham; and Abraham returned to
his place.*

—Genesis 18:20–33

This is an abbreviated example of what an intercessor does. An Intercessor is one who will wrestle with a person or an issue until there is a breakthrough. You can also look at Jacob wrestling the angel until He would bless him, found in Genesis 32. That was an intercession for a personal blessing.

*Then Jacob was left alone; and a Man wrestled with
him until the breaking of day. Now when He saw that
He did not prevail against him, He touched the socket
of his hip; and the socket of Jacob's hip was out of joint
as He wrestled with him.*

And He said, "Let Me go, for the day breaks."

But he said, "I will not let You go unless You bless me!"

So He said to him, "What is your name?"

He said, "Jacob."

*And He said, "Your name shall no longer be called
Jacob, but Israel; for you have struggled with God and
with men, and have prevailed."*

—Genesis 32:24–28

The New Testament Church

Peter was therefore kept in prison, but constant prayer was offered to God for him by the church. And when Herod was about to bring him out, that night Peter was sleeping, bound with two chains between two soldiers; and the guards before the door were keeping the prison. Now behold, an angel of the Lord stood by him, and a light shone in the prison; and he struck Peter on the side and raised him up, saying, "Arise quickly!" And his chains fell off his hands. Then the angel said to him, "Gird yourself and tie on your sandals"; and so he did. And he said to him, "Put on your garment and follow me." So he went out and followed him, and did not know that what was done by the angel was real, but thought he was seeing a vision. When they were past the first and the second guard posts, they came to the iron gate that leads to the city, which opened to them of its own accord; and they went out and went down one street, and immediately the angel departed from him.

And when Peter had come to himself, he said, "Now I know for certain that the Lord has sent His angel, and has delivered me from the hand of Herod and from all the expectation of the Jewish people."

So, when he had considered this, he came to the house of Mary, the mother of John whose surname was Mark, where many were gathered together praying. And as Peter knocked at the door of the gate, a girl named Rhoda came to answer. When she recognized Peter's voice, because of her gladness she did not open the gate, but ran in and announced that Peter stood before the gate. But they said to her, "You are beside yourself!" Yet she kept insisting that it was so. So they said, "It is his angel."

Now Peter continued knocking; and when they opened the door and saw him, they were astonished. But motioning to them with his hand to keep silent, he declared to them how the Lord had brought him out of the prison. And he said, "Go, tell these things to James and to the brethren." And he departed and went to another place.

—Acts 12:5–17

Here is a wonderful example of intercession working. The church was praying for Peter and his deliverance. They were praying throughout the night, and God heard their pleas and sent an angel to free Peter from a deep prison. When I say deep, I mean many layers. First, he was bound with two chains between two soldiers. Second, there were guards (plural) post by the locked door. Then there was a second guard post and an iron gate. An angel appeared and lit up the prison, stooped down and hit Peter on the side and raised him up. OK, hold it, have you ever been awakened in the middle of the night by some sort of alarm or noise? That panicked awakening where you're not sure where you are or what's happening? That's exactly what is happening here with Peter. The angel is barking out orders: "Gird yourself, tie on your sandals." "Wa- what? Oh OK, tie on my gird and wait, what?" Peter does his best to follow instructions and finds himself outside before it dawns on him that this all really happened. Peter then heads toward a place where he knew the church would be meeting and knocked on the door. When Rhoda came to answer the door, she recognized Peter's voice, but in her excitement she forgot to open the door. Others didn't believe it was Peter but said it was his angel. They did eventually let Peter in and re- joiced that their prayers were answered and God did deliver Peter from the hands of Herod.

I really want us to back out a little and take a look at some- thing. I say this tongue-in-cheek, but God miraculously broke chains, caused guards to sleep through an escape, opened at least two sets of doors and brought Peter out of a prison . . . but He couldn't get him into the church. The point I am making is not to criticize the church, but rather accept and recognize how much God can do outside the church. If we accept our roles, we can see God doing so much more around our every- day lives.

Contemporary Example of an Intercessor: The ICU Prayer Warrior

Scenario:

Premature twins, Luke and Levi, are fighting for life in the Neonatal ICU. Machines beep, alarms blare, and doctors warn their parents: "Prepare for the worst." The parents are too traumatized to pray.

Intercessor Action:

Dorothy (the babies' grandmother and a woman of deep faith) steps in.

- Spiritual Triage: Rallies a 24/7 prayer chain across five churches, assigning specific hours (Psalm 139:16). Anoints each incubator with oil, while whispering Scripture: "You formed their inward parts" (Ps. 139:13).
- Physical Presence: Sits silently between their incubators for hours, knitting prayer blankets—one stitch per silent petition.
- Battle in the Heavenlies: Disarms fear with worship: Plays "Great Is Thy Faithfulness" on her phone when doctors deliver grim updates.

Breakthrough:

- Day 7: Luke's lung hemorrhage inexplicably stops mid-transfusion.

- Day 21: Levi overcomes sepsis after 104.5-degree fever spiked then vanished.
- Nurses later admitted: "Something shifted in that room."

Why This Embodies an Intercessor:

- Fights unseen battles. "We wrestle not against flesh and blood" (Eph. 6:12). Dorothy targeted spiritual strongholds of fear and death.
- Stands in the gap. She bore the parents' burdens when they couldn't pray (Exodus 17:12).
- Prays with authority, not anxiety. Worship weaponized the atmosphere against despair.

True Intercessors:

- See beyond circumstances to God's throne room (Isaiah 6:1–5).
- Wield the prayer weapons God provides (2 Cor. 10:4).
- Persist until the spiritual atmosphere shifts (Daniel 10:12–13).

An Intercessor is heaven's shock absorber—receiving the impact of hell's fury and dissipating it through knees bent, hands lifted, and a heart anchored in the Unshakable.

These five biblical roles of AMBASSADOR, MEDIATOR, PEACEMAKER, ADVOCATE, and INTERCESSOR, are critical roles each believer can step into as they prayerfully navigate times of conflict. Rather than allowing conflict avoidance to betray our calling, we cannot allow the pressures of culture to silence us. There's a saying, "The only thing a good person needs to do for evil to dominate is NOTHING." The practice of private prayer, in the presence of God's holiness re-orients us, revives us, re-purposes us and transforms us into those who are not afraid to run into conflict with wisdom and confidence through the power of the Holy Spirit.

In the next chapter, we'll explore how Jesus embodies each of these five roles as a perfect example to us for biblical conflict management.

CHAPTER 3: JESUS IS OUR ULTIMATE EXAMPLE

What we will see here is how Jesus does not expect us to do anything that He has not done first. All five of these roles are sequentially positioned to bring a clear understanding and insight as to what each role looks like and how it operates. As we look to each role we can use in biblical conflict management, we can look to Jesus as our ultimate example.

1. Jesus as AMBASSADOR

The concept of Jesus as an ambassador can be understood in the sense that He represents God to humanity, acting as a messenger and reconciler between God and mankind. While the Bible does not explicitly call Jesus an "ambassador" in the modern diplomatic sense, several scriptures highlight His role as God's representative, sent to bring God's message, authority, and reconciliation to the world. Below are some key scriptures that point to this idea:

> So Jesus said to them again, "Peace to you! As the Father has sent Me, I also send you."
>
> —John 20:21

This verse shows that Jesus was sent by the Father with a mission and He in turn, sends His disciples in like kind. His role as one sent by God reflects the idea of representing the Father's will and authority.

> Now then, we are ambassadors for Christ, as though God were pleading through us: we implore you on Christ's behalf, be reconciled to God.
>
> —2 Corinthians 5:20

While this verse directly refers to believers as ambassadors for Christ, it implies that Jesus is the ultimate representative of God. As the one who reconciles humanity to God, Jesus embodies the role of an ambassador and His followers continue with Him in His mission.

> For God did not send His Son into the world to condemn the world, but that the world through Him might be saved.
>
> —John 3:17

Jesus was sent by God with a purpose—to save the world. This act of being "sent" reflects His role as a divine representative or ambassador of God's love and salvation.

> *Therefore, holy brethren, partakers of the heavenly calling, consider the Apostle and High Priest of our confession, Christ Jesus.*
>
> *—Hebrews 3:1*

The term "Apostle" means "one who is sent." Here, Jesus is explicitly called an apostle, indicating that He was sent by God as a representative to accomplish God's redemptive plan.

> *And the Word became flesh and dwelt among us, and we beheld His glory, the glory as of the only begotten of the Father, full of grace and truth.*
>
> *—John 1:14*

As the Word made flesh, Jesus represents God to humanity in the most direct way possible. He embodies God's message and presence, acting as the ultimate ambassador of the Father's will.

> *Let this mind be in you which was also in Christ Jesus, who, being in the form of God, did not consider it robbery to be equal with God, but made Himself of no reputation, taking the form of a bondservant, and coming in the likeness of men. And being found in appearance*

as a man, He humbled Himself and became obedient to
the point of death, even the death of the cross.

—Philippians 2:5–8

Jesus, though equal with God, humbled Himself to become human, so that He could represent God's love and plan of salvation. His incarnation and obedience reflect His role as God's representative to humanity.

He who receives you receives Me, and he who receives
Me receives Him who sent Me.

—Matthew 10:40

Jesus explicitly links Himself as the one sent by God, indicating that accepting Him is equivalent to accepting God. This underscores His role as a divine ambassador.

These scriptures collectively paint a picture of Jesus as the ultimate representative of God, sent to humanity to reveal God's nature, to proclaim His message, and to reconcile the world to Himself. While the term "ambassador" may not be used directly for Jesus, His mission and actions align with the concept of representing and speaking on behalf of God. Additionally, as stated in 2 Corinthians 5:20, the idea of believers being "ambassadors for Christ" flows directly from Jesus' own role as God's sent representative.

2. Jesus as MEDIATOR

The role of Jesus as a mediator—someone who stands between God and humanity to reconcile and facilitate a relationship—is a central theme in the New Testament. Below are key scriptures that highlight Jesus as a mediator between God and mankind:

> *For there is one God and one Mediator between God and men, the Man Christ Jesus.*
>
> *—1 Timothy 2:5*

This verse explicitly identifies Jesus as the sole mediator between God and humanity, emphasizing His unique role in bridging the gap caused by sin.

> *But now He has obtained a more excellent ministry, inasmuch as He is also Mediator of a better covenant, which was established on better promises.*
>
> *—Hebrews 8:6*

Jesus is described as the mediator of a new covenant, superior to the old covenant under the Mosaic Law. His mediation brings a better relationship with God based on grace, truth and forgiveness.

> *And for this reason He is the Mediator of the new covenant, by means of death, for the redemption of the transgressions under the first covenant, that those*

who are called may receive the promise of the eternal
inheritance.

—Hebrews 9:15

This verse again underscores Jesus' role as the mediator of
the new covenant, securing eternal redemption through His
sacrificial death.

To Jesus the Mediator of the new covenant, and to the
blood of sprinkling that speaks better things than that
of Abel.

—Hebrews 12:24

Jesus' mediation through His blood establishes a new relationship with God, surpassing the old covenant and offering
forgiveness and peace.

What purpose then does the law serve? It was added
because of transgressions, till the Seed should come
to whom the promise was made; and it was appointed
through angels by the hand of a mediator. Now a me-
diator does not mediate for one only, but God is one.

—Galatians 3:19–20

While this verse refers to Moses as an intermediary for the
law, it sets the stage for understanding Christ as the ultimate
mediator who directly reconciles humanity to the one true
God, as implied in the broader context of Galatians.

Therefore the law was our tutor to bring us to Christ, that we might be justified by faith. But after faith has come, we are no longer under a tutor. For you are all sons of God through faith in Christ Jesus.

—Galatians 3:24–26

Jesus said to him, "I am the way, the truth, and the life. No one comes to the Father except through Me."

—John 14:6

Jesus declares Himself as the only way to access God the Father, positioning Him as the essential mediator for salvation and relationship with God.

Therefore, having been justified by faith, we have peace with God through our Lord Jesus Christ, through whom also we have access by faith into this grace in which we stand, and rejoice in hope of the glory of God.

—Romans 5:1-2

Jesus is the means through which believers gain access to God and experience peace with Him, fulfilling the role of a mediator.

For through Him we both have access by one Spirit to the Father.

—Ephesians 2:18

Through Jesus, both Jews and Gentiles have access to God, highlighting His role as a mediator in uniting all people to the Father through the Spirit.

> *For it pleased the Father that in Him all the fullness should dwell, and by Him to reconcile all things to Himself, by Him, whether things on earth or things in heaven, having made peace through the blood of His cross.*
>
> —*Colossians 1:19–20*

Jesus' work of reconciliation through His death on the cross demonstrates His role as a mediator, restoring peace between God and creation.

These scriptures collectively affirm Jesus' unique and indispensable role as the mediator between God and humanity. Through His life, death, and resurrection, He reconciles sinners to a holy God, establishes a new covenant, and provides the only means of access to the Father. His mediation is rooted in His identity as both fully God and fully man, enabling Him to represent both parties perfectly.

3. Jesus as PEACEMAKER

Jesus as a peacemaker is a significant theme in the New Testament, reflecting His role in bringing reconciliation between God and humanity, as well as fostering peace among people. Below are key scriptures that highlight Jesus as a peacemaker, emphasizing His work in establishing peace through His life, teachings, death, and resurrection.

Now the fruit of righteousness is sown in peace by those who make peace.

—James 3:18

The reason Jesus brought peace was because He brought righteousness. His sacrifice at Calvary was to appease the righteous requirements of the Law that declared the penalty for sin is death. He did a righteous thing by paying the price for the sins of all the world.

Blessed are the peacemakers, For they shall be called sons of God.

—Matthew 5:9

In the Sermon on the Mount, Jesus teaches the value of peace-making as a characteristic of God's children. As the ultimate Son of God, Jesus embodies this principle, modeling and enabling true peace.

For He Himself is our peace, who has made both one, and has broken down the middle wall of separation, having abolished in His flesh the enmity, that is, the law of commandments contained in ordinances, so as to create in Himself one new man from the two, thus making peace, and that He might reconcile them both to God in one body through the cross, thereby putting to death the enmity. And He came and preached peace to you who were afar off and to those who were near.

Ephesians 2:14–17

Jesus is explicitly called "our peace," having reconciled both Jews and Gentiles to each other and to God through His death on the cross and His resurrection removing the hostility caused by sin and division.

> For it pleased the Father that in Him all the fullness should dwell, and by Him to reconcile all things to Himself, by Him, whether things on earth or things in heaven, having made peace through the blood of His cross.
>
> —Colossians 1:19–20

Jesus makes peace between God and creation through the sacrifice of His blood on the cross, demonstrating His role as the ultimate peacemaker.

> Therefore, having been justified by faith, we have peace with God through our Lord Jesus Christ.
>
> —Romans 5:1

Through Jesus, believers are justified and experience peace with God, ending the enmity caused by sin. His mediation establishes this spiritual peace.

> Peace I leave with you, My peace I give to you; not as the world gives do I give to you. Let not your heart be troubled, neither let it be afraid.
>
> —John 14:27

Jesus offers a unique, divine peace to His disciples, distinct from worldly peace. This reflects His role as a peacemaker who calms hearts and minds through His presence and promises.

> *For unto us a Child is born,*
> *Unto us a Son is given;*
> *And the government will be upon His shoulder.*
> *And His name will be called*
> *Wonderful, Counselor, Mighty God,*
> *Everlasting Father, Prince of Peace.*
>
> *—Isaiah 9:6*

This Old Testament prophecy about the Messiah refers to Jesus as the "Prince of Peace," foretelling His role in bringing peace to the world through His reign and redemptive work.

> *Glory to God in the highest,*
> *And on earth peace, goodwill toward men!*
>
> *—Luke 2:14*

At Jesus' birth, the angels proclaim peace on earth, signaling that His coming initiates God's plan for peace and goodwill toward humanity through His life and sacrifice.

> *Then, the same day at evening, being the first day of*
> *the week, when the doors were shut where the disciples*
> *were assembled, for fear of the Jews, Jesus came and*

stood in the midst, and said to them, "Peace be with you."

—John 20:19

After His resurrection, Jesus repeatedly greets His disciples with "Peace be with you," demonstrating His role as the source of peace, calming their fears and affirming His victory over death.

The word which God sent to the children of Israel, preaching peace through Jesus Christ—He is Lord of all.

—Acts 10:36

Peter declares that Jesus is the source of the "good news of peace," emphasizing His mission to bring reconciliation and harmony through the gospel.

Now all things are of God, who has reconciled us to Himself through Jesus Christ, and has given us the ministry of reconciliation, that is, that God was in Christ reconciling the world to Himself, not imputing their trespasses to them, and has committed to us the word of reconciliation.

—2 Corinthians 5:18–19

Jesus' work of reconciliation is central to His role as a peace-maker. Through Him, God reconciles the world, establishing peace by forgiving sins and restoring relationships.

These scriptures collectively portray Jesus as the ultimate peacemaker, who not only teaches and models peace, but accomplishes it through His sacrificial death and resurrection. He brings peace between God and humanity by atoning for sin, peace among people by breaking down barriers of hostility and inner peace to individuals through His presence and promises. His title as the "Prince of Peace" and His actions throughout His ministry affirm this vital aspect of His identity and mission.

4. Jesus as ADVOCATE

The concept of Jesus as an advocate refers to His role as one who intercedes, pleads, or speaks on behalf of believers before God the Father. The term "advocate" is explicitly used in some translations and contexts, often tied to the Greek word *parakletos*, which can mean helper, comforter, or intercessor. Below are key scriptures that point to Jesus as an advocate, highlighting His role in representing and supporting believers in their relationship with God.

My little children, these things I write to you, so that you may not sin. And if anyone sins, we have an Advocate with the Father, Jesus Christ the righteous.

—1 John 2:1

This verse directly calls Jesus an "Advocate" (Greek: *parakletos*), emphasizing His role in interceding for believers when they sin. As the righteous one, He pleads their case before the Father, securing forgiveness through His sacrifice.

For Christ has not entered the holy places made with hands, which are copies of the true, but into heaven itself, now to appear in the presence of God for us.

—Hebrews 9:24

Jesus appears in God's presence on behalf of believers, acting as their representative and advocate in the heavenly realm after completing His atoning work.

And I will pray the Father, and He will give you another Helper, that He may abide with you forever—the Spirit of truth, whom the world cannot receive, because it neither sees Him nor knows Him; but you know Him, for He dwells with you and will be in you. I will not leave you orphans; I will come to you.

—John 14:16–18

Although this verse refers to the Holy Spirit as another "Helper" (or "Advocate," *parakletos*), Jesus implies His own role as an advocate by promising to ask the Father on behalf of His disciples.

> "I pray for them. I do not pray for the world but for those whom You have given Me, for they are Yours.
>
> —John 17:9
>
> "I do not pray for these alone, but also for those who will believe in Me through their word; that they all may be one, as You, Father, are in Me, and I in You; that they also may be one in Us, that the world may believe that You sent Me.
>
> —John 17:20–21

In His High Priestly Prayer, Jesus intervenes for His disciples and future believers, advocating for their unity and protection. This prayer demonstrates His role as an advocate who pleads for His followers before the Father.

These scriptures collectively illustrate Jesus' role as an advocate who represents, and pleads on behalf of believers before God. His righteous character enables Him to effectively advocate for humanity, ensuring their forgiveness, protection, and access to God's grace. The term *parakletos* and related concepts of mediation and intercession underscore this vital aspect of His ministry.

5. Jesus as INTERCESSOR

The role of Jesus as an intercessor refers to His act of standing between God and humanity, praying, pleading, or intervening on behalf of believers from His heavenly position at the right hand of the Father. Below are key scriptures that point to Jesus as an intercessor, highlighting His intercessory ministry through His life, death, resurrection, and heavenly role.

> *Therefore He is also able to save to the uttermost those who come to God through Him, since He always lives to make intercession for them.*
>
> *—Hebrews 7:25*

This verse explicitly states that Jesus continually intercedes for those who approach God through Him. His eternal priesthood ensures ongoing intercession, securing complete salvation for believers.

> *Who is he who condemns? It is Christ who died, and furthermore is also risen, who is even at the right hand of God, who also makes intercession for us.*
>
> *—Romans 8:34*

Jesus, positioned at the right hand of God after His resurrection, actively intercedes for believers, protecting them from condemnation and representing their needs before the Father.

For Christ has not entered the holy places made with hands, which are copies of the true, but into heaven itself, now to appear in the presence of God for us.

—Hebrews 9:24

Jesus appears before God in heaven on behalf of believers, an act of intercession that ensures their representation and access to God's grace after His atoning work.

And the Lord said, "Simon, Simon! Indeed, Satan has asked for you, that he may sift you as wheat. But I have prayed for you, that your faith should not fail; and when you have returned to Me, strengthen your brethren."

—Luke 22:31-32

Jesus specifically tells Peter that He has prayed for him in the face of Satan's attacks, interceding for Peter's faith to endure. This personal intercession shows Jesus' care for individuals.

Therefore I will divide Him a portion with the great,
And He shall divide the spoil with the strong,
Because He poured out His soul unto death,
And He was numbered with the transgressors,
And He bore the sin of many,
And made intercession for the transgressors.

—Isaiah 53:12

This Old Testament prophecy about the Suffering Servant, points to Jesus and highlights His role in interceding for sinners, even as He bears their sins through His death.

These scriptures collectively affirm Jesus' role as an intercessor who actively prays and pleads on behalf of believers before God the Father. His intercession is rooted in His position as the eternal High Priest, His sacrificial death, and His exalted place at God's right hand. Whether through direct prayer during His earthly ministry or His ongoing intercession in heaven, Jesus continually represents and supports His people, ensuring their salvation and spiritual well-being.

Jesus perfectly fulfills all these roles:

- Ambassador – Came from the Father to manifest His glory.
- Mediator – Took on flesh to be both Son of God and Son of Man.
- Peacemaker – Died on the cross to pay the price for our sins.
- Advocate – Resurrected to bring man back to his redeemed relationship with God.
- Intercessor – Seated at the right hand of the Father forever making intercession for us.

CHAPTER 4: POWER, LOVE, AND A SOUND MIND

Therefore I remind you to stir up the gift of God which is in you through the laying on of my hands. For God has not given us a spirit of fear, but of power and of love and of a sound mind.

—2 Timothy 1:6-7

I hope we can see that the work of reconciliation is of God and that as believers we have the Holy Spirit in us working toward bringing redemption in times of conflict. We should not be afraid in this regard. It is obvious by our study that the biblical persons noted have been taking their place in these five roles of Ambassador, Mediator, Peacemaker, Advocate, and Intercessor and especially as seen in Christ Jesus. But it is important that we have a clear understanding and expectation regarding our involvement with conflict . . . WE ARE NOT ALONE. The power inspiring us, motivating us, and empowering us is the Holy Spirit and the Word of God. God is all about reconciliation, and we should be as well. A caveat to this is that by the same Spirit that will prompt you to operate in these roles will be the same Spirit leading you not to.

> Now when they had gone through Phrygia and the re-gion of Galatia, they were forbidden by the Holy Spirit to preach the word in Asia. After they had come to Mysia, they tried to go into Bithynia, but the Spirit did not permit them. So passing by Mysia, they came down to Troas.
>
> —Acts 16:6–8

Just as in the instance of Barnabas leaving with John Mark, only at a later time, was Paul to be reconciled to John Mark. Timing is everything, and that is why before we march into a situation where angels fear to trod, we have prayed and asked for not only the leading of the Lord, but the love and power of the Lord as well. I believe the "sound mind" comes when we recognize which role we are to pursue:

Ambassador – We are entering as a representation of God's kingdom, power, and glory. It is not about us or our feelings; it is about what His Word has to say about it. This is a solid footing and assurance that God is with us for the purpose of making Himself known.

Mediator – We are getting involved in a dispute between conflicted parties. We are neutral in that we represent both sides of the conflict. Our focus is to help them see through their limited perspective or one of self-defense. Helping them see that the "US" is more important than the "I."

Peacemaker – I believe this to be the most difficult, yet most important. The peacemaker brings the solution, solves the problem, and contributes substantially to the remedy. This is the wisdom of God, that "Aha!" breakthrough moment. Count on this to even surprise the one who is speaking it. It is a gift from the Holy Spirit. Do not forget this one can cost you.

Advocate – This role involves standing up for the underdog, the disadvantaged, the disqualified, those who cannot defend themselves and have no voice. This takes great courage and conviction. I believe conviction comes from being fully convinced in a person or cause. This is an unwavering stance that fortifies and protects the "least among us."

Intercession – Picture this process by comparing similar words. An *interception*, if you have ever watched an American football game, is when the team's momentum is heading in one direction and a member of the opposing defensive team catches a pass intended for the offensive team member. The direction and momentum of the game has radically shifted to the opposite direction. *Intersection* is where two roads cross at the same location . . . they intersect. Intercession can be compared to both by seeing a situation going in one direction and through prayer, counseling, or just interrupting, turns that direction toward redemption and reconciliation.

Embracing the Call to Transformative Conflict Engagement

We have journeyed through the profound reality of standing in the gap, much like a shock absorber between the unyielding Rock of Jesus Christ and the harsh Hard Place of the world. From personal stories of overwhelming pressure to biblical examples of courage and faith, we've explored how God calls us to engage in conflict, not with fear or avoidance, but with purpose and power. The five roles—Ambassador, Mediator, Peacemaker, Advocate, and Intercessor—offer us a framework to navigate tensions, bring reconciliation, and represent God's kingdom in a broken world. These roles, exemplified by figures like Joseph, Moses, Abigail, Esther, Peter, Barnabus, Paul and ultimately Jesus Himself, remind us that we are not alone in this mission. The Holy Spirit equips and guides us, providing the love, power, and sound mind needed to step into conflict with divine wisdom and grace.

As we have seen, conflict is not something to shy away from, but is often an opportunity to manifest God's redemptive work. Whether we are representing His truth as Ambassadors, facilitating dialogue as Mediators, solving disputes as Peacemakers, defending the voiceless as Advocates, or interceding through prayer and burden-bearing as Intercessors, we are called to be agents of transformation. Jesus, our ultimate example, perfectly embodied all these roles, showing us that standing between a rock and a hard place is exactly where we belong—absorbing the shocks of a fallen world while pointing others to the hope of His eternal kingdom.

Call to Action: Now is the time to rise up and embrace your role in transformative conflict engagement. Reflect on the areas of tension in your life —be it in your family, workplace, community, or even within yourself —and ask God to reveal which of these five roles He is calling you to embody. Stir up the gift of God within you, as 2 Timothy 1:6–7 urges, and step boldly into the fray, trusting that you are not driven by a spirit of fear, but by power, love, and a sound mind. Commit to being a shock absorber, standing in the gap with prayer, wisdom, and action. Start small if needed —mediate a disagreement, advocate for someone in need, or intercede fervently for a broken situation —but start now. The world desperately needs believers who will not hide from conflict, but will engage it with the heart of Christ. Will you say, "Yes, Lord" and take your place between The Rock and a Hard Place today?

You stand daily between the Rock of Ages and a world shattered by sin. Will you be a passive observer —or a shock absorber deployed by heaven? The five roles are your toolkit. Start where you are now: Intercede for one broken relationship. Advocate for one oppressed voice. Make peace in one warzone of bitterness. As you do, you will fulfill Ezekiel's vision: You will be the one who "stands in the gap" (Ezekiel 22:30).

DEEP GLIMPSES SERIES

Having served in full-time ministry for over thirty-three years, I have delivered countless sermons and teachings. While many of these messages blur together, a select few stand out as profound revelations—insights that have left an indelible mark on my soul and fundamentally changed my life.

These messages emerged from personal transformative experiences and comprise the books featured here in the Deep Glimpses series.

Remembering Communion

Jesus instructed, "Do this in remembrance of me." As you approach communion, what do you remember? I identified a direct parallel between marriage and communion, noting that the elements we remember about marriage correspond directly to our relationship with Christ and one another. Furthermore, I believe that the Lord's Table should involve more interaction among believers, making the presented pattern inclusive and participative.

The Appliance Gifts

God bestows grace upon each of us, connecting us through gifts that serve the church by strengthening, encouraging, and serving one another. These gifts function much like household appliances, contributing to a healthy and whole spiritual habitation.

The Author of Authority

In addition to being a pastor, I also led worship, fostering a dynamic culture within our worship experiences. However, there came a time when I questioned the direction and purpose of our focus in worship. Worship is far more than mere performance; it is a venue for exchange, impartation, and endowment. Understanding this can profoundly enhance the power in our lives.

Between the Rock and a Hard Place

I often felt overwhelmed with ministry tasks such as counseling, leadership meetings, and sermon preparation, while balancing my marriage and family. In desperation, I cried out to the Lord, "I feel like I'm between a rock and a hard place. His response was, "That's where you should be," and He showed me biblical positions to help equip me in making the most of those times.

Lord willing, there will be other books in this series, but for now my prayer is that you will be strengthened and encouraged with these insights and brought into a clearer understanding of your walk with the living God.

www.ingramcontent.com/pod-product-compliance
Lightning Source LLC
Chambersburg PA
CBHW071339130626

46556CB00004B/1946